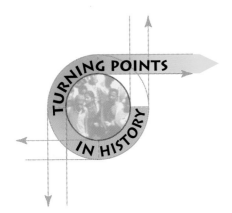

TURNING POINTS IN HISTORY

The end of apartheid
A New South Africa

RICHARD TAMES

Heinemann
LIBRARY

www.heinemann.co.uk
Visit our website to find out more information about **Heinemann Library** books.

To order:
☎ Phone 44 (0) 1865 888066
▤ Send a fax to 44 (0) 1865 314091
▯ Visit the Heinemann Bookshop at www.heinemann.co.uk to browse our catalogue and order online.

First published in Great Britain by Heinemann Library, Halley Court, Jordan Hill, Oxford OX2 8EJ, a division of Reed Educational and Professional Publishing Ltd. Heinemann is a registered trademark of Reed Educational & Professional Publishing Limited.

OXFORD MELBOURNE AUCKLAND JOHANNESBURG BLANTYRE GABORONE IBADAN PORTSMOUTH NH (USA) CHICAGO

© Reed Educational and Professional Publishing Ltd 2000
The moral right of the proprietor has been asserted.

Designed and map artwork by Robert Sydenham
Illustrations by Robert Sydenham, Ambassador Design
Originated by Ambassador Litho Limited
Printed in Hong Kong

ISBN 0 431 06919 0
04 03 02 01 00
10 9 8 7 6 5 4 3 2 1

British Library Cataloguing in Publication Data
Tames, Richard, 1946–
The end of Apartheid: a new South Africa. – (Turning points in history)
1. Apartheid – South Africa – Juvenile literature
2. South Africa – Politics and government – 1994 – Juvenile literature
I. Title
968'.065

Acknowledgements
The Publishers would like to thank the following for permission to reproduce photographs: Art Publishers: p. 8; Baileys African History Archives: p. 15; Bridgeman Art Library: (Stapleton Collection UK) p.7; Corbis: (AFP) p. 27, (Hulton-Deutsch) p. 19, (Charles OíRear) p. 21, (Reuters Newmedia Inc) p. 29, (David Turnley) p. 17, (Peter Turnley) pp. 4, 11, 26, (Nik Wheeler) p. 5; Hulton Getty: p. 6; Hutchison Library: (Robert Aberman) p. 12, (Ingrid Hudson) p. 16; Magnum Photos: p. 20; Rex Features: pp. 18, 23; (Ian McIlgorm), p. 25, (Sipa Press) pp. 14, 24, 28; Tames, Richard: pp. 9, 22.

Cover photograph reproduced with permission of Link Picture Library.

Our thanks to Christopher Gibb for his help in the preparation of this book.

Every effort has been made to contact copyright holders of any material reproduced in this book. Any omissions will be rectified in subsequent printings if notice is given to the Publisher.

Contents

Some words are shown in bold, **like this**. You can find out what they mean by looking in the Glossary.

A scrap of paper

Pushing a folded piece of paper into a big box is not particularly exciting – unless you have been waiting all your life for the right to do it. When the paper carries a cross against the name of a politician or party to govern your country, it really matters. Until 1994, three out of four South Africans had never been allowed to vote in an election in their lives. Then, on 27 April that year, millions of people lined up quietly, to follow the example of a tall man with a warm smile, grey-haired but still upright and fit at the age of 76 – Nelson Mandela.

The 1994 election made Nelson Mandela South Africa's first black president. A year later he published the story of his life, calling it *Long Walk to Freedom*. It was a good title. Mandela's long walk through life had taken him from barefoot cowherd to successful lawyer, from keen amateur boxer to dedicated champion of human rights, from student runaway to holder of 50 honorary degrees and the Nobel Prize for Peace, from 27 years in prison to hero of a continent.

Nelson Mandela's vital vote – 27 April 1994.

A vote for hope

Nelson Mandela chose to cast his vote in South Africa's first multi-racial elections at Ohlange High School, Natal, because that was where John Dube was buried. In 1912 Dube had founded the organization to which Mandela had given his life – the African National Congress. Before casting his vote, Mandela had laid a wreath on Dube's grave. When he did finally cast his vote 300 journalists were there to see him do it. Then he turned to them and said:

*'We are moving from an era of resistance, division, **oppression**, turmoil and conflict and starting a new era of hope, **reconciliation** and nation-building. I sincerely hope that the mere casting of a vote ... will give hope to all South Africans.'*

With the election of Mandela, the oppression of South Africa's black majority, which had sprung from the beginning of the state of South Africa itself, was coming to an end.

New nation, new flag.

THE UNITY FLAG

South Africa's new flag was adopted in 1994. The sideways 'V' into 'Y' shape represents groups in South Africa merging into unity as they move forward together. The six colours had been used in the various flags adopted during the course of South Africa's history.

Boer against Bantu

The first folk

In 1488 the Portuguese first rounded the Cape of Good Hope, sailing for India. Later, ships landed at the Cape, trading for food with people who called themselves Khoikhoi and lived by hunting and herding. Further inland the San (Bushmen) survived in very dry, desert country. Eastwards, in Natal, lived Bantu-speaking peoples, who were farmers as well as hunters and herders.

Dutch settlement

In 1652 the Dutch East India Company set up a base in southern Africa, to provide water and food for ships on their way to the East Indies. Ninety men, serving under Jan van Riebeeck, battled droughts, floods, insects, diseases and Khoikhoi cattle rustlers. Using slaves from other parts of Africa and the East Indies, they cleared land for crops.

By 1662 there were 250 white settlers, mostly Dutch with some Germans. In 1685 inter-racial marriages between white settlers and local black slaves were banned. Soon afterwards French **Huguenot** settlers joined the whites. When the British arrived later, European settlers who were already there became known as **Boers.** By 1707 there were 1779 whites and 1107 slaves.

A Boer family with black servants.

Moving inland

With the advantage of their guns, the Europeans took more and more Khoikhoi land. They were aided in this by European diseases, to which the Khoikhoi had no resistance. In 1713 smallpox wiped out many Khoikhoi, easing European movement inland.

By 1795, 15,000 whites and 17,000 slaves were scattered throughout the Cape colony, over an area twice the size of England, or roughly equal to Colorado. Cape Town was the colony's only town and port. Around it was land taken over by Boers, who raised cattle and whose slaves produced wheat and wine. Beyond that, the Boer population extended 600 kilometres (375 miles) inland, living by herding and farming. They killed the San, and enslaved their children. In 1779–81 Boers fought their first frontier war against Bantu-speakers. The Bantu-speakers lived in large tribes, and had iron weapons and so were better organized to fight.

This Zulu warrior is Utimuni, nephew of Shaka, the Zulu king.

AN AFRICAN NAPOLEON

While European settlers were pushing inland from the south-west, Dingiswayo (died 1817), leader of the Bantu-speaking Zulu, founded a powerful kingdom in Natal. His successor, Shaka (1787–1828), organized an army of 40,000 Zulu into *impi* (regiments) of superbly trained warriors. Shaka's wars of conquest started a wave of tribal migrations throughout southern Africa – called the *Mfecane* (crushing) – as weaker peoples fled his power. Although the Zulu empire was crushed by the British and the Boers, the memory of its strength remained to frighten many whites and inspire many Africans.

British and Boer

Struggle over slavery

As a result of wars that started in Europe, Britain took over the Dutch Cape colony in 1806, and sent settlers soon after that. In 1833 Britain ended slavery throughout its empire, including the Cape. The **Boers** wanted to keep their independence, believing they had a God-given right to own African land and slaves. So they began a 'Great **Trek**' inland, far from British rule.

The monument at Pretoria commemorating the Great Trek includes a circle of stone wagons modelled on the ones the trekkers used.

In 1838 they killed 3000 Zulus at Blood River, as they fought their way into Natal and avenged the murder of their leader Retief and his men. In 1843 Britain took over Natal, so many Boers moved even further inland to found the Orange Free State and Transvaal as independent republics.

Struggles over riches

In 1867 diamonds were discovered in Boer territory. *Uitlanders* (foreigners), mostly British, flooded in, soon outnumbering the Boers but, as foreigners, they had no vote. Some also hated the way the Boers treated African slaves. In 1877 the British tried to take over Transvaal, but they were resisted successfully. In 1886 gold was found in Transvaal, bringing in more unwanted fortune-hunters.

A second British–Boer war broke out in 1899. Boer forces were successful until the British built up a much bigger army. The Boers then used hit-and-run **guerrilla** methods. The British responded by forcing Boer families off their farms and into camps, to stop them giving Boer fighters food and information. The camps were badly organized and 26,000 Boer women and children died from disease and under-feeding. Although this was not intentional, it made many Boers bitter against the British.

In 1902 the Boers finally agreed to accept British rule, while keeping the **Afrikaans** language for their schools and courts, and receiving cash for damage to their farms. In 1910 Britain tried to reconcile the defeated Boers by joining the Cape, Natal, Orange Free State and Transvaal into one Union of South Africa – with the Boers effectively in control.

This statue of the South African leader, Jan Smuts, stands in Parliament Square, London.

ENEMY INTO FRIEND

Jan Smuts (1870–1950) was a Boer, who had been educated in Britain. Although he was a brilliant commander against the British, he still believed the Boers' best future lay in working with them. Smuts led South African forces for Britain in both world wars, serving in the British war cabinet both times and as South Africa's Prime Minister in 1919–24 and 1939–48. He also helped found the **United Nations.**

Whose country?

One country, many peoples

Despite being united under one government in 1910, South Africans remained deeply divided. Only 21.5 per cent of the population were white. Of these, an English-speaking minority dominated government and business in the cities, while the majority were **Afrikaans**-speaking **Boers**, mostly farmers and many still bitter about the war. The majority black population (67 per cent) was divided among many peoples. Some of these were large, such as the Zulu or Xhosa of the Transkei region, who spoke similar Bantu languages. Other groups were much smaller.

Whatever their tribe or language, black Africans had already lost the best lands to white farmers and businesses who used money, the law or brute force to take them. By 1910, black Africans owned less than 10 per cent of a country that their ancestors had completely controlled. In 1913 the South African Parliament passed a Native Land Act which limited ownership of land by blacks even more. There were also Indian immigrants (2.5 per cent) and 'coloureds' (9 per cent), born of mixed marriages between blacks and whites. Indians and coloureds had varying rights in the Cape, but were not treated as equals by most whites.

The Union of South Africa in 1910. The neighbouring countries are named as of 1910, with their present names in brackets.

SOUTHERN RHODESIA (ZIMBABWE)

BECHUANALAND (BOTSWANA)

GERMAN SOUTH-WEST AFRICA (NAMIBIA)

TRANSVAAL (SOUTH AFRICAN REPUBLIC)

PORTUGUESE EAST AFRICA (MOZAMBIQUE)

Atlantic Ocean

N

Pretoria

Johannesburg

Sharpeville

SWAZILAND

Orange Free State

Bloemfontein

Natal

BATSUOTOLAND (LESOTHO)

Durban

Cape Province

Indian Ocean

Umbata (Mandela's Birthplace)

AFRICA

Cape Town

Port Elizabeth

South Africa

0 km	1000 km
0 miles	620 miles

Getting organized

In 1912 the South African Native National Congress was founded to unite black Africans and defend their interests. Its anthem *Nkosi Sikelel'i Afrika* (God Bless Africa) is now South Africa's national anthem. From 1923 this organization became the African National Congress (ANC).

In 1913 James Hertzog (1866–1942), a former Boer general, formed the Nationalist Party to defend **Afrikaner** interests. He wanted South Africa to be completely independent from Britain.

War

When World War I broke out, Hertzog wanted South Africa to stay out of it. Some Boers took the chance to revolt against British rule. Prime Minister Louis Botha (1862–1919), the former top Boer commander, put down the revolt and conquered the neighbouring German colony of South West Africa. Like Smuts, he favoured **reconciliation** between Boer and Briton. The war also boosted South African industry and mining.

The flag of the African National Congress. The three colours represent black for the people, green for the land and gold for resources.

NEW WAYS TO FIGHT

Indians came to South Africa as labourers. Some prospered, becoming traders, but most were treated as second-class citizens by whites. Indian lawyer Mohandas Gandhi (1869–1948) founded the Natal Indian Congress to defend their rights. Here he began to develop the non-violent methods of political struggle (such as strikes, sits-in and **boycotts**) that he later used to free India itself from British rule. Indians called him *Mahatma* (Great Soul). Gandhi's ideas were later followed by Dr Martin Luther King Jr in the USA, and by Nelson Mandela in South Africa.

The roots of apartheid

Migrant labour

The wartime boom encouraged black African men to leave their families on the poor lands, in 'native reserve' areas set aside for them, and find work in mines and cities. They came back home periodically, bringing money they had earned. African **migrant** labour was needed permanently by industry, but Africans were regarded as only temporary residents outside the reserves. They were made to carry passes so that police could control their movement and check who had a job and therefore the right to be outside a reserve.

THE BROTHERHOOD

In 1918 some **Afrikaners** formed the *Broederbond* (Brotherhood) as a secret society to fight for the interests of Afrikaners as a separate nation. Members of the *Broederbond* came to hold important positions in politics, the army, the police and business, and used their power to help each other.

When the men were away, the women and children had to work the land alone.

War ends – troubles begin

The wartime boom was followed by hard times. In 1920 African mineworkers went on strike and African demonstrators were killed by police in Port Elizabeth. Against this background of troubles, a South African **Communist** Party was founded in 1921. Uniquely at that time, it accepted all races.

In 1922 white miners went on strike to protect their right to have all the skilled jobs. Black Africans protested against the laws that made them carry passes.

New government – new laws

The Labour Party, supported by white miners, joined forces with the Nationalist Party and, in 1924, defeated the South African Party, which had ruled since 1910. The new Nationalist government, led by James Hertzog, made South Africa more independent of British control and favoured white – and especially Afrikaner – interests at the expense of blacks. South Africa dropped the Union Flag in favour of its own national flag and sent its own ambassadors to foreign countries. **Afrikaans** was confirmed as an official language alongside English. The colour bar in the workplace, which reserved skilled jobs for whites, was strengthened.

A government-owned steel works was built at Pretoria, increasing the importance of heavy industry and mining and providing more jobs for whites. An Immorality Act limited mixed marriages among races. In 1929 Afrikaners began to use a new word to describe this policy of racial separation – **apartheid** ('separateness').

The new 1927 flag of the Union of South Africa combined the British Union Flag with the flags of the Orange Free State and Transvaal, as a symbol of respect for both British and Boer traditions.

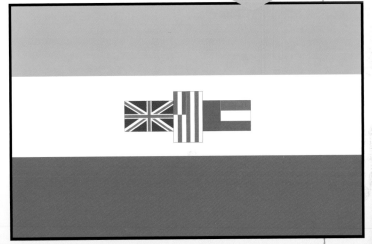

The counsellor's son

Herdboy

Nelson Mandela was born on 18 July 1918 in his family's **kraal** at Qunu, a village near Umtata, capital of the Transkei region. He was the son of the senior **counsellor** of the Paramount Chief of the Thembu tribe, but as a boy he still helped with herding cattle, which were his people's main form of wealth. Nelson also had the tribal name Rolihlahla, which in Xhosa means 'stirring up trouble'.

Runaway

Mandela went to schools run by white missionaries, then he went on to Fort Hare University College, where he met Oliver Tambo and became involved in student politics. He was suspended for his part in a protest about hostel food. The Paramount Chief ordered him to stop the protest, continue studying and marry a bride chosen for him. Instead Mandela ran away to Johannesburg and worked as a guard at a mine.

Nelson Mandela was a keen amateur boxer in his youth, and kept fit during his long years in prison.

Lawyer

In Johannesburg Mandela met Walter Sisulu, also from Transkei, who encouraged him to study and got him a job in a law office. Mandela studied law part-time at the University of Witwatersrand. He also joined Sisulu as a member of the African National Congress (ANC) and married Walter's cousin, Evelyn, a nurse.

Activist

Younger members of the ANC – including Sisulu, Tambo and Mandela – thought it was getting nowhere after 30 years of polite, peaceful protests. Some black Africans had the vote in Cape Colony, and ANC leaders had hoped it would gradually be given to black Africans in the rest of South Africa. Instead, in 1936, Hertzog's government limited black voting rights in the Cape to the choosing of three white **representatives.** As a result, in 1944, younger ANC members founded the ANC Youth League, intending to use more **militant** methods. In 1947 Mandela was elected secretary of the Youth League.

Mandela in the law office he shared with Oliver Tambo. It was the first black law firm in Johannesburg.

OLIVER TAMBO

Mandela's closest **comrades** in the ANC were also his lifelong friends. In 1952 Oliver Tambo (1917–93) joined Mandela to set up Johannesburg's first black law firm. Tambo later spent 30 years abroad representing the ANC, while Mandela was in prison.

Apartheid enacted

A turning point

World War II again boosted industry in South Africa, attracting even more black Africans to cities. Many whites feared that their jobs were threatened by Africans on much lower wages.

In 1948 they elected a Nationalist Party government under Dr Daniel Malan (1874–1959). He promised that the existing separation of black and white South Africans would become a total system of **apartheid.** This would officially classify people as whites, coloureds, Indians and Bantu (blacks). Each race would live in different areas, be educated separately, use separate transport, hospitals, libraries and cinemas and be forbidden to inter-marry.

A Suppression of Communism Act (1950) gave government the power to imprison anyone accused of favouring changes through 'disturbance or disorder'. In this way white privileges at work and white power in government would be protected for ever.

Separate and not equal – living conditions for blacks in a South African township.

Resistance

Resistance to apartheid through marches, strikes and **boycotts** was weakened by divisions among its opponents. Some ANC members favoured co-operating with other groups, such as **Communists** and organizations of Indians, coloureds or the white minority also opposed to apartheid. Others wanted a 'black Africans only' approach.

Separation of blacks and whites was enforced in public places such as beaches, where otherwise they might mix as friends.

Defiance

In 1950 Mandela was elected National President of the Youth League. With Sisulu he carefully planned a 'Defiance Campaign' of marches and meetings for 6 April 1952 – just as **Afrikaners** celebrated the 300th anniversary of Dutch settlement. Indians and some whites supported the campaign. The Nationalist government cracked down with arrests and made apartheid laws even harsher, but the campaign spread awareness of apartheid abroad, where it was condemned by the **United Nations.** It also boosted ANC membership from 7000 to over 100,000. Mandela was arrested under the Suppression of Communism Act, but he was not imprisoned because he had stressed the need to avoid any violence.

ARCHITECT OF APARTHEID

Dutch-born Hendrik Verwoerd (1901–66) was a sociology professor and editor of the Afrikaner daily newspaper *Die Transvaler.* He resigned from university in protest when South Africa admitted Jewish refugees from the Nazis. As Minister of Native Affairs (1950–8), Verwoerd drew up the detailed apartheid laws. Verwoerd became prime minister in 1958 and was **assassinated** in parliament in 1966 by a deranged, mixed-race messenger.

onfrontations

Banned!

Resistance to **apartheid** continued throughout the 1950s. The Nationalist government made strikes by Africans illegal and used banning orders to stifle over 1500 opponents. A person who was banned was forbidden to go to any meeting – defined as three or more people – or enter a court, college or newspaper office. Banned people could not be quoted or even contact each other. Banning orders, lasting from two to five years, could be renewed repeatedly.

In 1952 the ANC elected Chief Albert Luthuli as President-General, with Mandela as his deputy. Mandela was soon forced to resign when he became a banned person. In 1955 the ANC adopted a Freedom Charter calling for a non-racial South Africa, with equal rights for all.

In good company – Nelson Mandela stands in the middle of the third row from the front at the 1956 treason trial.

Trials and troubles

In 1956 Mandela, Tambo, Sisulu and over 150 others – 105 African, 23 white, 21 Indian, 7 coloured – were put on trial for alleged treason. The trial dragged on for four years. As defendants were free when they were not actually needed in court, Mandela continued working as a lawyer. After divorcing Evelyn, he married Winnie Nomzamo Madikizela, a friend of Tambo, in 1958.

In 1959 Chief Luthuli called for a foreign **boycott** of South African goods, to put pressure on the Nationalist government. In the same year a group within the ANC, opposed to co-operating with Indians and **Communists,** broke away to form the Pan Africanist Congress (PAC).

Sharpeville, after the shooting stopped.

Massacre

In 1960 the PAC organized a protest against the pass laws at Sharpeville (65 kilometres/40 miles south of Johannesburg, near Vereeniging). Some 5000 unarmed protesters gathered outside a police station. Stone-throwing led to shooting. At the end of the day 69 Africans were dead and 178 wounded. The ANC called for a national day of mourning. The government declared a State of Emergency, banned both ANC and PAC and imprisoned Mandela along with 2000 other anti-apartheid **activists.** Oliver Tambo fled abroad to set up ANC offices wherever it was safe.

Mandela used his treason trial to explain, 'We are not anti-white, we are against white supremacy'. In March 1961 he was found not guilty of treason. Later that year South Africa became a republic and left the **Commonwealth** rather than abandon **apartheid.** The ANC responded by forming a military wing – *Umkhonto we Sizwe* (Spear of the Nation) – to launch a **sabotage** campaign.

Struggling on

Fake independence

In 1959 a Bantu Self-Government Act planned **bantustans** under African chief ministers. Between 1976 and 1981 four of these 'homelands' – Transkei, Bophuthatswana, Venda and Ciskei – were recognized by South Africa as 'independent' states. In practice, they were too poor to support themselves. They relied on South Africa and money from their so-called citizens, who went to work in South Africa, leaving their families living in squalor. The bantustans were situated in some of South Africa's harshest areas. No other country recognized their independence.

Pressures outside and in

In 1962 South Africa made **sabotage** a **capital offence.** From 1967 being accused of **terrorism** could mean prison without trial. In 1974 a revolution in faraway Portugal suddenly brought independence to its former colonies, Mozambique and Angola. Zimbabwe became independent in 1981.

Pass books were needed to enforce apartheid. Destroying one was an act of defiance – and a crime. Unlike sabotage, this form of resistance needed no training or equipment.

These 'front-line states' had previously supported South Africa. Now, ruled by black majorities, they provided bases from which **guerrillas** of *Umkhonto we Sizwe* attacked economic targets, such as power stations. South Africa sent troops to raid the front-line states and eventually became involved in fighting in Namibia as well. South African military spending rose almost tenfold.

Many countries answered Luthuli's call, **boycotting** South African goods. South African teams were banned from the 1964 Olympics and international cricket and rugby. In 1974 South Africa was banned from the **United Nations** (UN) **General Assembly**.

The prisoner

When the ANC was banned in 1960, Mandela went on the run, visiting Ethiopia and Britain to rally support, then Algeria for military training. He was arrested in 1962, after secretly returning to South Africa, and was imprisoned for five years for organizing strikes.

In 1963 South African police arrested Sisulu and others at a secret *Umkhonto* base at Rivonia, near Johannesburg. Mandela was linked to their sabotage campaign and in 1964 he was sentenced to life imprisonment. As Prisoner 466/64 he was put to hard labour on Robben Island, allowed only one letter and one visit every six months. In 1973 Mandela was offered a shorter sentence if he would support the bantustan programme. He refused.

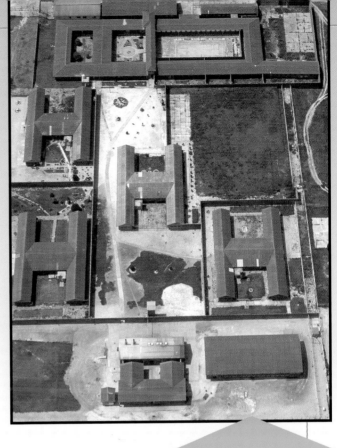

Robben Island Prison, viewed from above. Mandela was held in this grim place from 1964 to 1982.

SOWETO – MASSACRE OF SCHOOLCHILDREN

Soweto (the name was formed from SOuth-WEst TOwnships) is the southern, black area of Johannesburg. In June 1976, black schoolchildren there protested against being taught in **Afrikaans,** not English, because Afrikaans was regarded as the language of pass laws, permits and police. Police shooting and further riots killed over 500. Thousands fled to join *Umkhonto*, the military wing of the ANC. Plans for compulsory schooling in Afrikaans were dropped in the aftermath of Soweto. In 1977 the UN banned sales of weapons to South Africa.

South Africa under siege

Prison progress

In 1980 the **United Nations** called on South Africa to release Mandela and start 'meaningful discussion of the future of the country'. There were no discussions but Robben Island prisoners were allowed newspapers and to buy groceries and toiletries with money they earned gardening. Mandela and other 'special section' prisoners no longer had to break rocks to mend roads, or collect seaweed. In 1982, Mandela, Sisulu and three more Rivonia men were switched to Pollsmoor Maximum Security Prison, Cape Town, where they had radio and better food but were even more closely shut up. Mandela was, however, now the world's most famous prisoner and between 1979 and 1986 received awards from India, Austria, Venezuela, Cuba, East Germany, Britain, the USA, Spain, Sweden and Malaysia.

Divide and conquer?

Boycotts and **sabotage** continued. In 1983 the United Democratic Front was formed by 600 anti-**apartheid** organizations, to support the Freedom Charter. To split this opposition the government gave coloureds and Asians limited political rights. However, nearly all of them rejected their new rights, and demanded rights for everyone, regardless of race. In 1985 the ban on mixed marriages was ended. By then military spending had risen hugely, to 4800 million Rand, and the army had almost doubled again, to 639,000. This meant heavy taxes and a strong military presence, which made foreign businesses nervous of **investing.**

Honouring the prisoner – this statue was unveiled in London in 1984, the twentieth year of Mandela's imprisonment.

"THE STRUGGLE IS MY LIFE"
NELSON MANDELA
GAOLED 5th AUGUST 1962
SENTENCED TO LIFE IMPRISONMENT
12th JUNE 1964 FOR HIS ACTIONS
AGAINST APARTHEID

ERECTED BY THE GREATER LONDON COUNCIL
UNVEILED BY OLIVER TAMBO
PRESIDENT OF THE AFRICAN NATIONAL CONGRESS
28th OCTOBER 1985

State of emergency

Concessions to coloureds and Asians only made black South Africans even more determined to struggle for their rights. The government offered Mandela early release if he would condemn ANC **militant** tactics. He refused. Rioting and school boycotts led to a State of Emergency being declared from July 1985 to March 1986. There were 8000 arrests and 750 deaths. Overseas the USA and France led trade and investment **sanctions** on South Africa, which cost it between 32 and 42 thousand million US dollars between 1985 and 1989.

A voice to be heard – Archbishop Desmond Tutu, who won the Nobel Peace Prize for his work against aparthied.

DESMOND TUTU (1931–)

Desmond Tutu, the son of a Transvaal teacher, also taught in schools before becoming an Anglican priest. He rose rapidly to become the first black Anglican Bishop of Johannesburg (1985–6). Although he still opposed violence, he repeatedly risked imprisonment by calling for strong sanctions against South Africa. In 1984 Tutu won the Nobel Peace Prize. This prize is awarded annually by Norway to the person or organization that has done most for human rights. In 1986 he became Archbishop of Cape Town. In 1995, after apartheid had been overcome, he began to chair the Truth and **Reconciliation** Commission, which uncovered political and police crimes that had been committed under apartheid.

A new beginning

Reassurance

In May 1988 the **UN** called again for Mandela's release without conditions. Mandela himself wrote to South African President P. W. Botha suggesting that 'the meeting between the government and ANC will be the first major step towards peace in the country'. Mandela insisted that South Africa should remain one country where everyone had equal rights, rather than be divided into **bantustans** and areas for other races. He also insisted that 'majority rule will not mean domination of the white minority by blacks'.

Possibly the biggest birthday party in the world, held at Wembley, London, in 1988 – and Mandela, the guest of honour, was in prison, so he couldn't attend.

THE BIGGEST BIRTHDAY

In 1988 Mandela's 70th birthday was honoured by a massive concert in London's Wembley Stadium. It was attended by 75,000 people, and watched on television by a billion more in 64 countries. Eleven mailbags of birthday cards were delivered to his wife Winnie at Mandela's Soweto home.

Momentous meetings

In July 1989 President Botha at last met Mandela briefly, both men pledging 'support for peaceful developments'.

Mandela with President F. W. de Klerk.

Botha had recently suffered a stroke, and in August resigned on grounds of ill health. This opened the way for a new approach by a new leader. In September Botha was succeeded as president by F. W. de Klerk. The new president was determined to break out of what he recognized as an endless 'cycle of violence', in which riots provoked crack-downs which provoked more riots. A month later, on his orders, Walter Sisulu and seven other political prisoners were released – to a tumultuous welcome.

De Klerk and Mandela at last met face to face in December. Mandela declared de Klerk to be 'the most honest and serious white leader he had come across'. On 2 February 1990 de Klerk announced the end of the ban on the ANC, the PAC, the Communist Party and over 30 other anti-**apartheid** organizations.

Free at last!

On 11 February 1990, after 27 years in prison, Nelson Mandela walked out, a free man. That same day he declared, 'Today the majority of South Africans, black and white, recognize that apartheid has no future.' Chris Hani, deputy commander of *Umkhonto we Sizwe*, observed, 'I think we're going to learn from him that we need to be better South Africans – to forgive and forget and to look forward …'

The ending of apartheid

Reforms

The State of Emergency, which had been renewed every year since 1986, ended in 1990. In 1991 laws enforcing **apartheid** were abolished. In Johannesburg **representatives** of political, church and business groups met, as the Convention on a Democratic South Africa (CODESA), to discuss a new democratic **constitution.** A majority of white voters now supported de Klerk's moves away from the past and towards a new future. But not everybody did.

Conflicts...

Not surprisingly, white **Afrikaner** extremists opposed the ending of apartheid. So did many members of the security forces who feared past illegal actions might be punished. The PAC resented the dominant role of the ANC. The strongest opposition, however, came from the Inkatha Freedom Party (IFP) led by Chief Buthelezi, whose followers clashed violently with ANC supporters.

Nelson Mandela taking the oath of office, as President of South Africa, 10 May 1994.

Strikes, demonstrations and two mass-killings led to a temporary breakdown of CODESA. Talks – this time including the PAC – finally resumed in April 1993, only to be interrupted by the **assassination** of ANC leader Chris Hani. In June, Inkatha walked out of the talks.

...and compromise

CODESA plans for moving by stages to a multi-racial system were rejected by a Freedom Alliance (FA) of Inkatha, the Ciskei and Bophuthatswana governments and the **Afrikaner** *Volksfront* of hard-line Afrikaner groups. Intense discussions and **compromises** finally persuaded the FA to take part in the April 1994 general elections. These resulted in a clear victory for the ANC and the inauguration of Nelson Mandela as President of South Africa.

CHIEF MANGOSUTHU BUTHELEZI (1928–)

Buthelezi, a descendant of the Zulu royal house, became a chief at 25. He opposed apartheid, but in 1972 he became chief minister of the KwaZulu **bantustan** for fear of something worse being imposed. He also founded the Inkatha Freedom Party to organize support among Zulu tribesmen. Buthelezi's reluctant acceptance of bantustan office was bitterly opposed by ANC leaders. When apartheid ended Buthelezi wanted special rights for KwaZulu within any new political set-up. In the 1994 election Inkatha won control of the new province of KwaZulu/Natal and Buthelezi accepted the post of Home Affairs Minister in a government led by the ANC.

Chief Buthelezi addressing Inkatha supporters at a Soweto rally during the 1999 election campaign.

No easy walk to freedom

President, superstar

In 1993 Mandela was awarded the Nobel Peace Prize jointly with President de Klerk. Ever since his release, people all over the world have been deeply impressed by Mandela's immense dignity and charm, and his willingness to forgive those who had taken away 27 years of his life and liberty by keeping him in prison. Mandela believed that without a spirit of **reconciliation** between former enemies, no new South Africa could be created, and he set the example himself.

1994 was to prove a great year for the new South Africa. It rejoined the **Commonwealth** and joined the **Organization of African Unity.** International sporting links were renewed – a major step for a sport-mad nation that had been shut out of world competition for 30 years. South African cricketers and athletes made a storming comeback. In 1995 South Africa hosted and won the Rugby World Cup.

Nelson Mandela celebrating with the South African soccer team after they won the Africa Cup in 1996.

Facing the future

Nelson Mandela often quoted the Indian independence leader Nehru to warn his followers that there would be 'no easy walk to freedom'. The new South Africa still faces huge problems. Despite its immense riches in minerals, gold, diamonds and fertile soil, and despite being the biggest industrial power in Africa, the country is still blighted with poverty.

After Mandela – President Tabo Mbeki.

Unemployment stood at 30 per cent in 1998. Millions still live without electricity or running water. One in five of the population cannot read or write. High hopes had been raised by the ending of **apartheid** and could not be quickly satisfied. Years of violent political struggles have left a continuing problem of violent street crime. This in turn has made foreign businesses nervous of **investing** to create the new jobs that South Africa so badly needs.

But there have been major successes. With the ending of rule by armed force, the size of the military has more than halved. Former freedom-fighters from *Umkhonto we Sizwe* have been absorbed into a reformed army and police force. Most important of all is the fact that in 1999, when Nelson Mandela stepped down as president, Tabo Mbeki, his former deputy and old prison **comrade** from Robben Island, succeeded to the presidency smoothly and without any threat of political violence. Mandela's last gift to his country has been to bring it to the point where it could learn to do without him.

Time-line

1652	Jan van Riebeeck establishes Dutch East India Company settlement at the Cape
1806	British take over Cape Colony
1828	Death of Shaka, Zulu King
1834	Abolition of slavery in British-controlled territories
1838	Boers undertake Great Trek to the interior
1867	Diamonds discovered in Boer territory
1877–81	First Boer War confirms Boer independence
1886	Gold discovered in Transvaal
1899–1902	Second Boer War defeats Boer republics
1910	Formation of Union of South Africa
1912	South African Native National Congress established
1913	Land Act limits ownership of land by blacks; National Party founded
1914–18	World War I
1918	Birth of Nelson Mandela; *Broederbond* founded
1920	African miners' strike
1921	South African Communist Party founded
1922	White miners' strike
1924	Afrikaans recognized as an official language
1936	Black voting rights in Cape Colony limited
1939–45	World War II
1944	ANC Youth League founded
1948	Nationalist Party government elected
1950	Suppression of Communism Act passed
1952	ANC launches Defiance Campaign
1955	ANC adopts Freedom Charter
1956	Mandela charged with treason
1959	Chief Luthuli calls for foreign boycott of trade with South Africa Bantu Self-Government Act passed
1960	ANC banned; police kill 67 demonstrators at Sharpeville
1961	South Africa leaves the Commonwealth and becomes a republic
1964	Mandela sentenced to life imprisonment South Africa banned from Olympics
1966	Prime Minister Dr Hendrik Verwoerd is assassinated
1976	Soweto uprising
1977	UN Security Council bans arms sales to South Africa
1984	Desmond Tutu awarded Nobel Peace Prize
1985	South African government ends ban on mixed marriages
1988	Mandela's 70th birthday concert at Wembley, England
1990	Mandela released
1991	Apartheid laws abolished
1994	Mandela inaugurated as President of South Africa on 10 May
1995	Truth and Reconciliation Commission established South Africa wins Rugby World Cup
1999	Tabo Mbeki succeeds Mandela as president

Glossary

activist	someone actively involved in supporting a cause, especially in politics
Afrikaans	form of Dutch spoken by Afrikaners
Afrikaner	white Boer native speaker of Afrikaans
apartheid	political programme to separate races
assassinate	murder, especially for a political purpose
bantustan	area set aside for African self-government
Boer	in Dutch literally means 'farmer'; a white of Afrikaner descent
boycott	refuse to have anything to do with a person or institution or to buy their goods
capital offence	crime punishable by death
Commonwealth	organization of former British colonies set up to help each other through trade, aid and training
communist	supporter of Communist Party, who in South Africa supported violent revolution to achieve government control of all farms and businesses, and the abolition of all other political parties
compromise	reach an agreement by giving up part of one's demands
comrade	fellow member of a political group
constitution	basic framework of rules about how a country is to be governed
counsellor	someone who gives important advice
General Assembly	United Nations body in which every country has an equal vote
guerrilla	someone who fights in small groups using hit-and-run methods
Huguenots	French Protestants; hundreds of thousands fled France when toleration of Protestantism ended in 1685
invest	put money into a business
kraal	South African village of huts surrounded by a fence
migrant	person who leaves home in search of work or a better way of life
militant	aggressive, willing to risk confrontation
oppression	harsh rule to crush opposition
Organization of African Unity	organization founded in 1963 to promote co-operation among African states, to end colonial rule in Africa and raise African living standards. South Africa joined in 1994.
reconciliation	making friends when there has been strong disagreement before
representative	someone who speaks on behalf of another person or group
sabotage	deliberate destruction, usually for a political purpose
sanction	form of punishment, such as refusal to trade
terrorism	acts of violence committed for political reasons
trek	'journey' in Afrikaans
United Nations (UN)	organization founded in 1945 to promote international co-operation, to which almost every country in the world belongs

Index

Titles in the *Turning Points* series include:

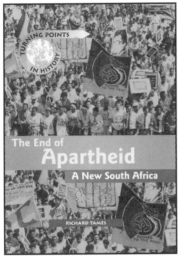

Hardback   0 431 06919 0

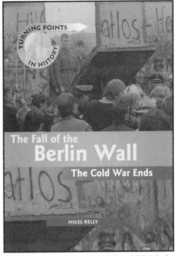

Hardback   0 431 06918 2

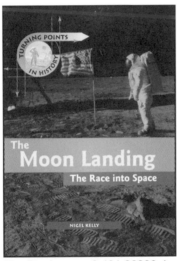

Hardback   0 431 06920 4

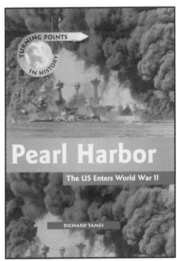

Hardback   0 431 06917 4

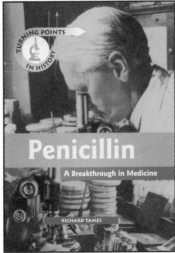

Hardback   0 431 06916 6

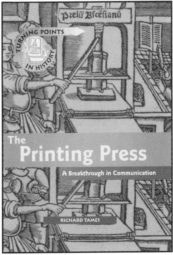

Hardback   0 431 06921 2

Find out about the other titles in this series on our website www.heinemann.co.uk/library